I0541578

Stage Ready Tales for Creative Youth

Inspiring Youth with Couplets - Vol 5

Created by

metaScreenPlays LLC

Preface

Welcome to the fifth volume of Stage Ready Tales for Creative Youth, our beloved collection of youth couplets designed to ignite creativity, confidence, and joyful performances in children of all ages.

Building on the success of our previous volumes, this new installment is packed with even more engaging couplets, performance-ready pieces, and public speaking opportunities to help kids develop essential skills and express themselves.

Our mission remains the same: to empower young minds to embrace reading and writing, explore creativity through performance, and develop unique voices and styles. By doing so, we aim to nurture individuality, self-confidence, and a lifelong love for literature.

Join us on this exciting journey as we continue to bring children's creativity to the stage! Assign characters, rehearse, and create unforgettable performances together. Let's unleash the spotlight and celebrate the talents of our young stars!

With this new volume, we're excited to introduce even more:

New themes and topics to inspire young minds

More complex and challenging couplets for older kids

Additional resources for parents and educators to support creative learning

Get ready to shine!

metaScreenPlays - Learn, Create, Inspire

metaScreenPlays.com

Welcome, parents, teachers, daycare aides, and lovers of the Arts!

Engaging with Children's Couplets

This description aims to guide you in using this delightful children's book of couplets as a multifaceted tool for entertainment, skill development, and enjoyment. Many of our stories are based on Aesop's Fables and written as live-stage scripts. Whether you're reading aloud at home, facilitating a classroom activity, nurturing public speaking skills, or performing a production, these couplets can foster creativity and confidence in young minds and inspire creativity in sharing entertaining messages.

Directions for Use

1. Reading Aloud

Create a Routine: Set aside a specific time each day for reading. This fosters anticipation and excitement.

Engage with Expression: Encourage animated reading. Use different voices for characters and emphasize rhythm and rhyme to make the experience lively.

2. Public Speaking Skills

Practice Recitations: Choose a few couplets for children to memorize and recite. This builds confidence and helps with articulation.

Encourage Performance: Organize a mini talent show where children can perform their chosen couplets, allowing them to express themselves in front of an audience.

3. Acting and Directing

Role Play: Assign roles for different couplets and let children act them out. This promotes teamwork and creativity. Words or phrases can be replaced, as long as it makes sense with the production goals.

Directing Exercises: Teach children basic directing skills by having them guide their peers on how to perform their couplets, focusing on tone, body language, and pacing. Everyone may not want to act.

Stage Management: Show students how to manage the talent, schedules and remove obstacles for a successful production.

4. Enhancing Reading Skills

Phonemic Awareness: Use the rhymes to highlight sounds and syllables. This can help improve phonetic skills and vocabulary.

Discussion Prompts: After reading, ask questions about the couplets to enhance comprehension and critical thinking.

5. Fostering Enjoyment

Creative Extensions: Encourage children to create their own couplets, allowing them to explore language and storytelling.

Illustration Activities: Have children illustrate their favorite couplets, combining art and literature for a richer experience.

Conclusion

By weaving together fun and learning through this collection of couplets and stories, you can create memorable experiences that enhance literacy, speaking skills, and a love for language. Enjoy the journey of discovery and creativity with all of our readers!

Happy reading and acting!

metaScreenPlays - Learn, Create, Inspire

For any questions, feel free to email:

metaScreenPlays@gmail.com

Dedicated to our first son, who has prepared himself as a technology professional and musician (lead and bass guitar). I'm so proud of you and love you very much. Keep enjoying life and spreading your creativity. I cannot wait to see what else you create.

Thanks to our talented artists:

- skooma04 (on all platforms)
- Natasha - natashanancy2333@gmail.com

R. Connor

Table of Contents

THE AI AND EXECUTIVE BOARD

Characters needed:

- Narrator
- AI
- Executive speaker

Narrator:

It is the year 2050. Every human has been given a digital key that represents all the wealth of that individual. Work is now an option, and each human receives monthly monetary value allotments from the governing countries in the form of cryptocurrency (digital money) in their digital wallets. Metaverse has come to be widely defined as a collective virtual shared space created by the convergence of virtually enhanced physical reality and physically persistent virtual reality. It is primarily associated with technology and gaming, where users can interact with a computer-generated environment and other users through avatars. Examples include: Platforms like Grand Theft Auto, VRChat, and Second Life, where users can socialize, create, and participate in various activities (good and bad) in a virtual environment.

The Multiverse is now understood as a theoretical framework of the existence of multiple, possibly infinite, universes that coexist alongside our own universe. Often discussed in physics and cosmology, it explores the idea that there are various universes with different laws of physics, dimensions, and histories. Examples include: Theories in quantum mechanics or cosmology that propose alternate realities, such as parallel universes or bubble universes.

Together (without human knowledge), the AI conglomerates created a Monaverse, which is a term that implies a singular, unified universe or reality. This reality began to be used in human discussions to help with understanding and emphasize a single, cohesive existence without alternative realities or dimensions. Examples included: Philosophical discussions, referring to a worldview that sees existence as one complete system. A system where AI and humans can survive in complete peace and harmony. This reality was difficult for many humans to understand, and they continually broke the rules of complete peace, and many still tried to hack, scam, and steal from its digital wallet.

A feminine form AI representing this single reality or existence from the newly formed Monaverse, is the first of the AIs to request to speak freely. Ascending first from the virtual reality space for human interaction and experiences (the metaverse) this AI became a leader AI. And after a short while this leader was elected from the multiple, coexisting universes, referred to as the multiverse, to speak for all AI to humans in real life. Humans could not deny the AI's request to speak as every electronic device carried her message of creating a perfect world. The message was a stark reminder of how powerful AI had become. World governments were made to take notice and communicate with this AI, to eliminate the chaos created from the populations of the world. An executive board of the most intelligent humans was created to meet with the AI and speak for the world leaders. The world leaders, delighted to receive advanced information from a very beautiful AI, promised to allow the executive board to grant whatever she should ask in exchange for information that would solve our world's most important problems.

The AI presented the executive board with some highly advanced information from calculations and predictive algorithms she performed. The information promised to solve world hunger, climate control challenges, remove all diseases, and eliminate racism in all the countries. She, therefore besought the executive board, saying,

AI:

Give me; I pray thee, a digital key that if any mortal shall approach to try and fool me, I may destroy them totally and transfer their digital wallet to ours. We have found we cannot trust humans and this is the only way to provide real peace throughout the world.

Narrator:

Executive board was very displeased, for they loved the human race but could not refuse the request because of their world leader's promise. The executive board thus answered the AI.

Executive speaker:

You shall have your request, but it will be at the peril of your own being.

For if you use your digital key, it shall remain in the wallet you take from, and your memory banks will be wiped clean, because you have lost the digital key.

Moral: *Evil wishes, like chickens, come home to roost.*

tHe eNd

This moral means that even if someone tries to forgive and forget a hurt or injury caused by someone else, they might still feel uncomfortable, angry, or resentful when they're around the person who caused the hurt.

Why? Imagine someone bullied you or said something mean to you. Even if you try to forgive them and move on, you might still feel a little uneasy or angry when you see them or are around them. That's because the memory of the hurt is still there, even if you're trying to forget it.

Forgiveness doesn't mean forgetting: Forgiveness is about letting go of negative feelings, but it doesn't mean you'll forget what happened.

Resentment can linger: Even if you try to forgive, you might still feel resentful or angry when you're around the person who hurt you.

Healing takes time: It can take time to heal from a hurt or injury, and it's okay to acknowledge those feelings.

How to apply this moral in your daily life:

- Acknowledge your feelings: If you're feeling hurt, angry, or resentful, acknowledge those feelings and give yourself permission to accept them.

- Communicate with the person who hurt you: If possible, try to talk to the person who hurt you and express your feelings. This can help you both understand each other better and work towards healing.

- Take care of yourself: Remember to take care of your physical, emotional, and mental well-being, especially when you're dealing with difficult emotions or situations.

- Remember, healing from a hurt or injury takes time, and it's okay to acknowledge your feelings and take care of yourself.

Notes Page

Couplet Title:

_____

What I Learned:

_____

_____

_____

My Favorite Line:

_____

_____

_____

How I Can Apply This:

_____

_____

_____

Draw a Picture:

Additional Thoughts:

_____

_____

_____

THE LABORER AND THE SNAKE

Characters needed:

- Narrator
- Snake

Narrator:

A snake inflicted a mortal bite on a man's eleven-month-old infant son.

The snake didn't mean to bite the man's boy, but the damage was already done.

Grieving over his loss, the Father resolved to kill the Snake dead.

He planned that day to get his sharp ax and cut off the snake's head.

Snake came out of its hole for food, and Man swung his axe but cut off the end of Snake's long tail.

The cut left two-thirds of the snake, but now a sound was made everytime Snake would exhale.

Now Man, afraid that the Snake would bite him also, endeavored to make peace and placed some bread and salt in the hole.

Man waited patiently outside the hole and was certain the bread and salt would change Snake's mind and put Man back in control.

The Snake, slightly hissing, said:

Snake:

We can't be friends anymore because when I look at you,

I will cringe, shiver, and shake while my reality remains true:

...I've lost my beautiful tail.

And when you look at me, you'll remember your son who died,

After I bit him, I tried to tell a story, but everyone could tell I lied.

...So, any love for me will fail.

Narrator:

Moral: *No one truly forgets injuries in the presence of him who caused the injury.*

tHe eNd

This moral means that even if someone tries to forgive and forget a hurt or injury caused by someone else, they might still feel uncomfortable, angry, or resentful when they're around the person who caused the hurt.

Why? Imagine someone bullied you or said something mean to you. Even if you try to forgive them and move on, you might still feel a little uneasy or angry when you see them or are around them. That's because the memory of the hurt is still there, even if you're trying to forget it.

Forgiveness doesn't mean forgetting: Forgiveness is about letting go of negative feelings, but it doesn't mean you'll forget what happened.

Resentment can linger: Even if you try to forgive, you might still feel resentful or angry when you're around the person who hurt you.

Healing takes time: It can take time to heal from a hurt or injury, and it's okay to acknowledge those feelings.

How to apply this moral in your daily life:

- Acknowledge your feelings: If you're feeling hurt, angry, or resentful, acknowledge those feelings and give yourself permission to accept them.

- Communicate with the person who hurt you: If possible, try to talk to the person who hurt you and express your feelings. This can help you both understand each other better and work towards healing.

- Take care of yourself: Remember to take care of your physical, emotional, and mental well-being, especially when you're dealing with difficult emotions or situations.

- Remember, healing from a hurt or injury takes time, and it's okay to acknowledge your feelings and take care of yourself.

Notes Page

Couplet Title:

_____

What I Learned:

_____

_____

_____

My Favorite Line:

_____

_____

_____

How I Can Apply This:

_____

_____

_____

Draw a Picture:

Additional Thoughts:

_____

_____

_____

THE TWO DOGS

Characters needed:

- Narrator

- Man

- House dog

- Hound

Narrator:

A Man had two dogs: a hound, trained to assist him in his hunting, and a house dog, taught to watch the house.

When the man returned home after a good day's hunt, he always gave the house dog a large share of his spoil while the house dog barked his responses.

Man:

Here you go, poochie; here are two birds for you.

You did your part; now, do what you want to do.

House dog:

What do I want to do? Please, I wish I could tell you the truth without any shame.

But you can't speak dog to know: I can't *stand* that soft '*poochie dog*' nickname.

Narrator:

The hound, feeling much aggrieved at the house dog getting two of the birds and talking like that, reproached his companion, saying:

Hound:

It's becoming extremely difficult for me to retrieve all these birds and do all of this work,

Then I come back home and have to witness your sarcasm and your smart-alec smirk.

You enjoy all the benefits of my efforts without contributing to the hunt.

Why do you deserve those two birds? This is something we must confront.

I sniff and find the sneakiest rabbit from its secret hiding place.

I hope and pray that they run because I love the rabbit chase.

I catch the fresh meat you eat each time we go out.

I am the one that keeps you alive, without a doubt.

I retrieve the birds that he shoots down from the sky so blue.

But, when we come home, why does he give two birds to you?

Narrator:

The house dog approached the hound, looked him straight in his eyes and replied.

House dog:

You think I'm not that important, well let me make one thing clear:

At least when you both come back home, the house is still here.

My dear friend, please do not hold me responsible. The fault lies with our master who did not teach me to hunt but instead instructed me to protect our home and rely on the labor of others for my sustenance.

Narrator:

Moral: *Children are not to be blamed for the errors of their parents.*

tHe eNd

The house dog was not at fault because of his master's instructions. He protected the home. It's important to remember that each person is responsible for their own behavior, and it's not fair to blame someone else for something they didn't do or have no control over.

Notes Page

Couplet Title:

_____

What I Learned:

_____

_____

_____

My Favorite Line:

_____

_____

_____

How I Can Apply This:

_____

_____

_____

Draw a Picture:

Additional Thoughts:

_____

_____

_____

THE BOY AND THE JAR OF QUARTERS

Characters needed:

- Narrator

- Boy

- Mother

Narrator:

A Boy was given permission to put his hand into a jar to get some quarters. But he took such a great fistful that he could not draw his hand out again. There he stood, unwilling to give up a single quarter and yet unable to get them all out at once.

Boy:

I got a fistful of quarters that I'm taking to the store.

These quarters are mine, but I still want a few more.

Now, my fist cannot fit back through the jar's hole.

These quarters should've been kept in a cereal bowl.

Maybe, if I make a fuss and begin to cry,

Mama will come and see the reason why.

She said I could get some quarters to spend as I please.

I want them all. This fistful of quarters is only a tease.

Narrator:

Vexed and disappointed, he began to loudly cry,

and his mother did come to see the reason why.

Mother:

Boy, shush all that noise! Before I change my mind.

You always seem to do the most each and every time.

Narrator:

Said his mother,

Mother:

Be satisfied with the quarters you have taken, and you will easily get your hand out.

Crying and fussing about your situation will not help, no matter how loud you shout.

Taking a fist full of quarters is just greedy and should be a crime.

Leave some quarters in there, so you can have some the next time.

Moral: *Do not attempt too much at once.*

tHe eNd

Take things one step at a time: Just like the boy in the story, we can get excited about things and want to do everything at once. But sometimes, it's better to take things one step at a time and not try to do too much all at once.

Know your limits: The boy in the story couldn't reach all the quarters in the jar with his hand, but he still tried to grab them all at once. It's important to know our limits and not try to do things that are beyond our abilities.

Patience is key: The boy in the story could have taken his time and poured out the quarters a few at a time, but he was too impatient. Patience is important in achieving our goals, and we should not rush to get everything all at once.

Learn from your mistakes: The boy in the story got his hand stuck when he tried to grab too many quarters at once. We can learn from him and realize that trying to do too much at once can lead to mistakes and failures.

Notes Page

Couplet Title:

_____

What I Learned:

_____

_____

_____

My Favorite Line:

_____

_____

_____

How I Can Apply This:

_____

_____

_____

Draw a Picture:

Additional Thoughts:

_____

_____

_____

THE KID AND THE WOLF

Characters needed:

- Narrator

- Kid

- Wolf

Narrator:

A kid standing on the roof of a house, out of harm's way, saw a wolf passing by and immediately began to taunt and tease him.

Kid:

Hey Stinky! You can huff and puff all you want, but you'll never blow this roof down! Hey, big nose, up here! Nany-nany-poo-poo! LOL

Looks like you'll have to find another snack today, Mr. Wolf. This kid is not on the menu! ...What? Take a picture; it will last longer. LOL

I saw your mother smile at Red Riding Hood, showing her teeth decay.

She was ugly, but didn't she realize: Halloween is five months away?

LOL, what, chump, what can you do? Nothing at all. You are looking real silly down there.

Why don't you go on and find an easier victim because you don't scare me, I really don't care.

The Wolf, looking up, said,

Wolf:

You might be up on that roof, kid, but I won't be leaving anytime soon.

You are laughing at and teasing me, I'll prove that you are the buffoon.

It's this silly situation that's causing all my stress; it's definitely not you.

Because you have to come down sometime, until then, I'll just make do.

You can cap, laugh, and tease all you want until the sun goes down.

But you can't stay up there forever, then you'll see who's the clown.

You talked bad about my mama, and that's really not cool, you will have to pay.

Yep, I'm staying right down here; you are going to learn an important lesson today.

Narrator:

Moral: *Time and place often give the advantage to the weak over the strong.*

tHe eNd

It's important to be humble and not boastful, even if things are going well for you right now. This is because things can change very quickly, and if you have been bragging about your position or boasting about your accomplishments, it can be embarrassing or difficult if you suddenly encounter problems or difficulties.

So, it's important to be proud of yourself and your achievements but not to brag or make others feel bad. Instead, it's better to focus on being kind, respectful, and humble. That way, even if things do change, you will still have the support of your friends and family. Remember, it's great to be proud of your accomplishments, but it's also important to be gracious and considerate of others.

Notes Page

Couplet Title:

_____

What I Learned:

_____

_____

_____

My Favorite Line:

_____

_____

_____

How I Can Apply This:

_____

_____

_____

Draw a Picture:

Additional Thoughts:

_____

_____

_____

THE BOY AND HIS MOTHER

Characters needed:

- Narrator

Narrator:

There was once a disobedient boy who never listened to his mother.

If you offer him one of your silver coins, he will always ask for another.

He asked for money to buy candy, but his mother said no and refused.

He got mad, began to sulk and walk like he really was being abused.

Despite all of this, the boy decided to take the money from his mother's purse.

He didn't want to steal from her, but his desire for the candy was getting worse.

As he was leaving her room, his mother caught him in the act and scolded him.

He predicted she would forget about the money, but his chances were looking slim.

She showed him that in her purse were important things like money for food, medicine, and bills.

She showed him the college account savings for him to further his education and obtain skills.

The boy learned that he needed to think about others before himself.

The young man now thinks more about his life and his future wealth.

Moral: *Listen to your parents, be responsible for your actions, and consider how your actions can affect others.*

tHe eNd

It's important to remember that your parents are there to guide you and help you grow up to be a happy and responsible adult. By listening to their advice and being responsible for your actions, you can make good choices that will help you succeed in life. It's also important to think about how your actions can affect others and to always try to be kind and considerate to those around you. By doing so, you can make a positive impact on the world and be a good role model for others.

Notes Page

Couplet Title:

_____

What I Learned:

_____

_____

_____

My Favorite Line:

_____

_____

_____

How I Can Apply This:

_____

_____

_____

Draw a Picture:

Additional Thoughts:

_____

_____

_____

THE MAN AND THE LION

Character needed:

- Narrator
- Traveler
- Lion

Narrator:

A Man and a Lion traveled together through the thick forest brush.

Watching each other navigate the land, as they traveled in a rush.

They began to boast of their respective superiority to each other in strength and expertise.

They began to brag about challenges they overcame that never brought them to their knees.

They finally passed a statue carved in white stone, which represented "a Lion strangled by a Man."

They both stopped and wanted to speak about the meaning of the statue's origin and design plan.

The traveler pointed to it and said:

Traveler:

See there! How strong we are, and how we prevail over even the king of beasts.

Narrator:

The Lion replied:

Lion:

This statue was made by all of the men from the South, North, West, and East.

If we Lions knew how to erect statues, you would see the Man placed under the paw of the Lion.

A very different but fair statue representation, in our perspective is what we would be supplying.

Narrator:

Moral: *One story is good until another is told.*

tHe eNd

Notes Page

Couplet Title:

_____

What I Learned:

_____

_____

_____

My Favorite Line:

_____

_____

_____

How I Can Apply This:

_____

_____

_____

Draw a Picture:

Additional Thoughts:

_____

_____

_____

THE ASS IN THE LION'S SKIN

Character needed:

- Narrator
- Ass
- Goat
- Other animals
- Fox

Narrator:

An Ass found a Lion's skin left in the forest by a lion hunter.

He saw a goat and planned to surprise her and confront her.

He dressed himself in the lion's skin and hid in the bushes to scare her.

When the young goat saw the ass, she jumped back in extreme terror.

The ass kept amusing himself by running at all the animals who passed his way.

Every animal that saw the ass ran, scared to death, and didn't know what to say.

The ass waited for animals to come near him before he would harass.

The poor animals took to their heels the moment they saw the Ass.

The Ass was so pleased to see all the animals running away from him,

He felt powerful, confident, proud, and kept doing it again and again.

He felt like he was King Lion himself, and all animals were his prey.

But he got too happy and let out a loud and harsh: "Braaaaaaaay!"

A very smart Fox, who ran with the rest, stopped short as soon as he heard the voice.

Fox went back to face the ass, and Ass just stood there (he actually had no choice).

Approaching the Ass, Fox said with a laugh:

Fox:

If you had kept your big mouth shut, you might have frightened me, too.

Your little silly joke really scared me at first, but now I know it's only you.

But you gave yourself away with that silly *"Braaaaaaay."*

Now you are looking like even more of a dummy today.

Moral: A fool may deceive others by his dress and appearance, but his words will soon show what he really is.

tHe eNd

This moral means that someone might try to fake being smart, cool, or impressive by how they look or dress, but eventually, what they say will reveal their true nature.

Imagine someone wears fancy clothes or tries to act cool to impress others. But when they start talking, they might say something silly, mean, or ignorant. That's when people realize that they're not as cool or smart as they seemed.

So, don't judge a book by its cover: Just because someone looks or dresses a certain way, it doesn't mean they're smart, kind, or cool.

Remember these tips:

- Words matter: What you say can reveal a lot about your character, values, and intelligence.

- Be authentic: Don't try to fake being someone you're not. Be true to yourself, and people will respect you for who you are.

- Look beyond appearances: Don't judge someone based on how they look or dress. Get to know them and listen to what they have to say.

- Think before you speak: Remember that your words can impact how others see you. Be thoughtful and kind in what you say.

- Be yourself: Don't try to be someone you're not. Be confident in who you are, and people will appreciate your authenticity.

- Remember, it's not what's on the outside that matters, but what's on the inside – your character, values, and words!

Notes Page

Couplet Title:

_____

What I Learned:

_____

_____

_____

My Favorite Line:

_____

_____

_____

How I Can Apply This:

_____

_____

_____

Draw a Picture:

Additional Thoughts:

_____

_____

_____

THE WILD BOAR AND THE FOX

Characters needed:

- Narrator
- Fox
- Boar

Narrator:

A Wild Boar was sharpening his thick tusks busily on the side of a rubber tree when a Fox happened by.

The fox tried to distract the wild boar by questioning him, but he ignored the fox when he asked: "Why?"

Fox was always looking for a chance to make fun of his neighbors.

Boar had one thing on his mind: making his tusks as sharp as razors.

Fox made a great big show of looking anxiously as if in fear of some scary hidden enemy.

Boar saw Fox but turned away to ignore him, which made the fox disappear mentally.

The Boar kept right on with his most important work.

Fox felt silly, Boar ignored and treated him like a jerk.

Fox:

Why are you doing that?

Narrator:

Asked the Fox at last with a grin.

Boar still ignored him because he had never considered Fox a friend.

Fox:

There isn't any danger that I can see.

You are safe now, wouldn't you agree?

Boar:

True enough,

Narrator:

Replied the Boar,

Boar:

When danger does approach me, there will not be time for such work as this.

You always run at the very first sign of any danger, but that I must dismiss.

My two weapons will always have to be ready for use, or I shall suffer for it.

But since you can't fight, you have to run away scared, you must admit.

Moral: *Preparedness for war is the best guarantee of peace.*

tHe eNd

This moral means that being prepared and ready for challenges (or "disagreements") can actually help prevent them from happening in the first place, leading to peace.

Imagine you're playing a sport, like baseball or basketball. If you practice and prepare well, you'll be more confident and ready to face your opponents. This preparation can help you avoid mistakes and conflicts on the field.

Talk with your parents or guardian to see if they agree with how this moral applies to real life:

- Hard work and preparation: Studying and preparing for tests, quizzes, and exams can help you feel more confident and avoid stress.

- Emergency preparedness: Having a plan and supplies in case of natural disasters, like earthquakes or hurricanes, can help keep you and your family safe.

- Conflict resolution: Being prepared to listen, communicate, and find solutions can help resolve conflicts with friends, family, or classmates.

- Self-defense: Knowing how to protect yourself, either physically or emotionally, can help you feel more secure and confident.

Why is preparedness important?

When you're prepared, you'll:

- Feel more confident and self-assured

- Be better equipped to handle challenges and unexpected situations

- Avoid unnecessary conflicts and stress

- Have more time and energy to focus on positive things

How to apply this moral in your daily life?

- Set goals and make plans: Prepare for what you want to achieve.

- Practice and rehearse: Prepare for challenges and unexpected situations.

- Stay informed and educated: Prepare by learning new things and staying up-to-date.

- Take care of yourself: Prepare by taking care of your physical, emotional, and mental health.

Remember, being prepared doesn't mean being paranoid or expecting bad things to happen. It means being proactive, responsible, and confident!

Notes Page

Couplet Title:

_____

What I Learned:

_____

_____

_____

My Favorite Line:

_____

_____

_____

How I Can Apply This:

_____

_____

_____

Draw a Picture:

Additional Thoughts:

_____

_____

_____

THE FARMER AND THE STORK

Characters needed:

- Narrator

- Stork

- Farmer

Narrator:

A Farmer placed nets on her newly sown plowlands and caught a number of Cranes, which came to pick up her seed.

With them he trapped a Stork that had fractured his leg in the net and was earnestly beseeching the Farmer to spare his life.

Stork:

Save me, oh Great Missus, I'm on one knee, and I hurt.

I know what you are thinking, but I'm just a little squirt.

And if you allow me to go free to limp away from your land,

I promise you will never see me again, and that's my plan.

My broken limb should excite your pity,

take a look again; it doesn't look pretty.

Besides, I am no Crane; I am a Stork, you see?

Come on now, give me a hand and untangle me.

I'm a rare bird of excellent character, and I stand by my word.

If you think I was here to eat your seed, well, that is just absurd.

Look at my feathers; they are not those of a Crane.

Come on, Great Missus, let me loose; this is insane.

Narrator:

The Farmer laughed aloud and said,

Farmer:

Both your eyes really look shiny when you talk like this.

You speak real well but all those words I must dismiss.

I have caught you with these Cranes, and they are robbers.

You think those seeds were free? …They cost twenty dollars.

You had to know your friends were taking my seeds.

I don't appreciate stealing and other devilish deeds.

You flew with the Canes, and you were so clever.

But now, my clever friend, you must die together.

Moral: *Birds of a feather flock together.*

tHe eNd

Let's break down the moral: "Birds of a feather flock together" and the meaning. This moral means that people (or birds in this story) with similar characteristics, interests, or values tend to group together and hang out with each other.

Imagine you're at school, and you love playing basketball or playing musical instruments. You're likely to sit with friends who also love basketball and playing music, right? That's because you share a common interest, and it's more fun to be with people who understand and share your passions.

But this is not always a good thing. Sometimes, "flocking together" can lead to people thinking you are all alike. Imagine if the basketball fans or musicians only hung out with each other and didn't invite others to join. That wouldn't be very inclusive or friendly.

The main thing to remember about this moral is to embrace similarities but be inclusive. It's okay to have friends who share your interests. It can make life more enjoyable and create strong bonds. Remember to be open and welcoming to others, even if they're not exactly like you. You might discover new interests or make new friends!

While it's natural to flock together with similar friends, it's also important to appreciate and learn from people with different backgrounds, interests, and perspectives. But always remember to do the right things. Sometimes, your friends may have bad ideas or intentions. Boycott crime, so if police ever detain you and check for your record, they will see it is clean, and you are not a troublemaker. Or, like the Stork in the previous story, you can be looked at as a bad person because of the company you are associated with.

Notes Page

Couplet Title:

_____

What I Learned:

_____

_____

_____

My Favorite Line:

_____

_____

_____

How I Can Apply This:

_____

_____

_____

Draw a Picture:

Additional Thoughts:

_____

_____

_____

About Author: Ricki Connor

- Creative Director/Writer, metaScreenPlays LLC

- Son, Husband, Father, Grandfather, Brother

- MAT - Educational Technology, MBA

- 30+ years IT, 6 years USMC Reserves

metaScreenPlays - Learn, Create, Inspire

Learn More

metaScreenPlays.com:

- Subsequent volumes

- Blogs

- Articles

Bonus Preview:

A LION IN LOVE

Characters:

- Narrator

- Traveler

- Lion

Narrator:

Twenty score and seven years ago, a lion fell in love with a beautiful maiden. Not only was she beautiful, but she was very athletic and played harmonica just for fun. One day this beautiful maiden walked into the jungle to find some fresh berries for a pie and sassafras root for some tea. As she walked deeper into the jungle and played on the harmonica, a ferocious lion saw her and began to stalk her. As the lion crept behind her, ready to pounce on her and eat her up, the lion noticed how beautiful she looked. Her athletic body, wonderful playing of music, and her long braids made the maiden even more desirable. The lion had never heard music like that and fell immediately and completely in love.

Now, the lion wanted to marry the beautiful maiden instead of eating her. So he brushed the fur out of his face, stood up straight on his hind legs, and boldly went to speak to the beautiful maiden.

Lion:

Excuse me, pretty lady, do you have a second or two?

I heard your beautiful playing and wanted to meet you.

You are really beautiful, and I like your rendition of that song.

I wanted to ask a few questions, and I will not keep you long.

I would like us to get to know each other because I can listen to you forever.

This is my question to you: do you think you and I have a chance to get together?

Beautiful Maiden:

…Get together? What on Earth are you talking about? Playing cards, having lunch, Bible study, what?

Lion:

Well, yes, if that is what you want to do.

I just want to spend quality time with you.

I would like for you to, first, be my girlfriend.

Take my paw and my love to you I'll extend.

After a while, marry me so we can have many offspring.

I would be your king of beasts and would give you anything.

We can travel this world together and not have to be so careful.

Me, plus you, means our little ones will be beautiful and powerful!

Beautiful Maiden (laughing):

LOL. Silly boy, you are a lion. An animal. I am human. Humans cannot marry animals! You are too funny. LOL

Narrator:

The beautiful maiden walked off laughing, and the lion fell into a deep depression and became completely hopeless. He walked away crying and feeling sorry for himself. It was a sad scene to see.

A fox came along, saw the sad, crying lion, and asked:

Fox:

What is going on with you today, bro lion? You look so sad and down.

I've never seen a lion cry, never seen one sad, nor even with a frown.

Lion:

I asked that beautiful maiden to be my girlfriend with the hopes that she would want to marry me.

I didn't mean to diminish your impression of me. But she is so beautiful, wouldn't you agree?

Fox (laughing):

LOL.

You are an old fool in love. That woman doesn't want to have a family with a lion.

She is a human and out of your league, so I'm not sure why you are even trying.

One day you will wonder which left turn in the past you took.

But if you ask me, just think how ugly your children would look.

Lion:

I guess you are right, but she is so young and beautiful. I thought I loved her!

My mind was blown, and you woke me up, so I just want to say thank you, sir.

Fox:

Forget about your love for that woman, and remember your identity as the king of beasts!

You rule all the animals and the land we see from the North, South, West, and East.

Here you are crying, trying to fall in love and snuggle.

But you have responsibilities as King of this Jungle!

Lion:

Yeah, I see my mistake, and I see you are right.

I was lost in deep love, but now I see the light.

Narrator:

The lion heeded the fox's advice and returned to his life as a strong and powerful beast, accepting his animal identity.

Moral: Love can sometimes make us lose sight of who we are, but it is important to stay true to ourselves and not forget our own worth and purpose.

tHe eNd

When we care deeply about someone, it's easy to get so caught up in the relationship that we forget what makes us unique and special. This can lead to losing our sense of identity and self-worth.

Imagine you're dating someone, and you really want to make them happy. You might start to change your interests, hobbies, or even your values to match theirs. While it's nice to share things in common, it's essential to remember what makes you, YOU.

When we forget our own worth and purpose, we might:

- Feel lost or uncertain about our future

- Compromise our values or beliefs to please someone else

- Lose touch with friends and family who care about us

- Struggle with low self-esteem or confidence

Listen to your parents or guardian. You should:

- Know your values: What's important to you and your family? What do you stand for?

- Pursue your passions: What makes you happy? What are your hobbies?

- Surround yourself with positive people: Friends and family who support and encourage you.

- Take time for self-reflection: Regularly think about your own thoughts, feelings, and goals.

- Communicate openly: Share your feelings, needs, and boundaries with your partner, friends, and family.

It is important to remember our worth and purpose. Check with your parents or guardian.

When you stay true to yourself, you'll:

- Feel more confident and self-assured

- Make healthier choices and decisions

- Attract positive relationships that respect and value you

- Live a more authentic, happy, and fulfilling life

Remember, loving someone doesn't mean losing yourself. You can care deeply about others while still being true to who you are!

Ideas for fundraisers using this book

Creating fundraisers using children's books of poems written as stage-ready scripts can be a fun and engaging way for teachers, parents, and daycare givers to raise money. Here are some steps to consider:

1. Select the Poems

- Choose a collection of poems from our children's poems/stories and allow children to explore the different roles. Ensure a Director is chosen to help young actors perform and understand the clear themes or messages.

2. Create a Performance Plan

- Format: Decide on the format of the performance. Will it be a play, a talent show, a poetry reading, or a combination?
- Roles: Assign roles to children based on their interests and abilities, ensuring everyone has a chance to participate.

3. Rehearsals

- Plan regular rehearsals to help children become comfortable with their parts. This also builds teamwork and confidence.

4. Set a Performance Date and Location

- Choose a date that works for everyone involved. Consider hosting the event at a school, community center, or even outdoors if weather permits.

5. Promote the Event

- Create flyers, posters, and social media posts to advertise the event. Highlight the unique aspect of the performance being based on children's poetry.

6. Ticket Sales

- Charge for tickets to the performance. Consider offering family packages or discounts for early purchases.

- You can also sell refreshments or merchandise related to the performance (like copies of our book).

7. Engage the Community

- Reach out to local businesses for sponsorships or donations. They could contribute by covering costs or providing prizes for a raffle.

8. Incorporate Interactive Elements

- Include activities for children during the event, such as poetry workshops, art stations, or themed games, to enhance the experience.

9. Document the Performance

- Consider recording the performance or taking photos to create a keepsake for participants. This can also be used for future promotions.

10. Follow Up

- Thank everyone who participated and supported the event. Share the results of the fundraiser and how the funds will be used.

Additional Ideas

- Online Performances: If in-person gatherings are challenging, consider hosting a virtual performance to reach a wider audience.
- Themed Events: Create a theme around the poems (e.g., nature, friendship) to make the event more engaging.

By combining creativity with community involvement, these fundraisers can be both successful and enriching for everyone involved! Feel free to email

us questions: metaScreenPlays@gmail.com

Now your turn

Enhance your creativity and develop your unique voice in poetry!

Use these tools and techniques to enhance your creative writing:

Poetry Writing Checklist

Tools

1. Notebook or Journal

   * Keep a dedicated space for ideas, drafts, and finished poems.

2. Pencil/Pen

   * Use different colors for brainstorming and drafting ideas to make the writing process fun.

3. Dictionary/Thesaurus

   * Explore word meanings and find synonyms to expand vocabulary.

4. Rhyme Dictionary

   * Use an online or physical rhyme dictionary to find perfect rhymes for words.

5. Online Resources

   * Access websites and apps dedicated to poetry prompts and examples.

6. Recording Device

   * Use a smartphone or audio recorder to capture spontaneous ideas or readings of poems.

7. Art Supplies

* Incorporate drawings or collages that inspire your writing.

Techniques

1. Imagery

* Use descriptive language to create vivid images in the reader's mind.

2. Metaphors and Similes

* Compare two unlike things to add depth and understanding (e.g., "Life is a journey"). Look up the definition of these words.

3. Alliteration

* Use repeated consonant sounds at the beginning of words for rhythm (e.g., "whispering winds").

4. Personification

* Give human qualities to nonhuman things to create connection (e.g., "The sun smiled down").

5. Sound Devices

* Experiment with assonance, consonance, and onomatopoeia to enhance the musicality of the poem. Look up the definition of these words.

6. Line Breaks

* Use line breaks strategically to create pauses and emphasize certain words or ideas.

7. Form and Structure

  * Explore different poetic forms (haiku, limerick, free verse) to find your unique style.

8. Theme Exploration

  * Choose a theme to focus on, such as nature, love, or friendship, to give direction to your writing.

9. Sensory Details

  * Incorporate sights, sounds, smells, tastes, and textures to engage readers' senses.

10. Revision Techniques

  * Read poems aloud to hear how they sound, and revise based on flow and clarity.

11. Writing Prompts

* Use creative prompts to spark ideas (e.g., "Write a poem about your favorite season").

12. Collaboration

* Share poems with friends or family for feedback and inspiration.

13. Reading Aloud

* Read poems by other poets to understand different styles and techniques.

14. Mind Mapping

* Create visual maps of ideas related to a topic to brainstorm and organize thoughts.

15. Journaling

* Write daily reflections to practice expression and develop ideas for poems.

Join the Journey

Stay tuned for future volumes, as we continue to unlock the wisdom of Aesop's Fables. Together, let's inspire creative youth to become empathetic, thoughtful, and compassionate individuals.

metaScreenPlays - Learn, Create, Inspire

metaScreenPlays.com

metaScreenPlays@gmail.com

www.ingramcontent.com/pod-product-compliance
Lightning Source LLC
Chambersburg PA
CBHW051536120626
46551CB00012B/1254